THE MARBLE QUEEN

HENRI COLE

THE
MARBLE
QUEEN

ATHENEUM

New York   1986

ACKNOWLEDGMENTS The author wishes to thank editors of the following publications, where poems, often in different form, first appeared: ANTAEUS: "V-Winged and Hoary"; "The Prince Enters the Forest" GRAND STREET: "Diana and the Adder"; "The Buoyant Ending" THE HUDSON REVIEW: "Dorothy's Fossils" THE NATION: "The Marble Queen"; "The Mare"; "Of Island Animals" POETRY: "Father's Jewelry Box" SHENANDOAH: "Patroclus: A Love Song"; THE SOUTHERN REVIEW: "Midnight Sailing on the Chesapeake." The author also wishes to thank the Ingram Merrill Foundation for financial assistance in completing this volume.

Library of Congress Cataloging-in-Publication Data

Cole, Henri.
    The marble queen.

    I. Title.
PS3553.04725M37   1986   811'.54   85-28701
ISBN 0-689-11779-5
ISBN 0-689-11796-5 (pbk.)

To my mother and father
and
to the memory of John P. Sawyer
(1952-1985)

Future joys are like tropic shores: out into the immensity that lies before them they waft their native softness, a fragrant breeze that drugs the traveler into drowsiness and makes him careless of what awaits him on the horizon beyond his view.

GUSTAVE FLAUBERT, *Madame Bovary*

Contents

THE MARBLE QUEEN

Lines on Seeing a Lock of Keats' Hair

Bittersweet as fall, magnificent fall,
the azure room where mercury youth dissolved,
sun-spurged beneath the brown-beamed, blossom-
blown ceiling, tiptop a plunge

of milky steps, dusty and foot-fretted, falling
into the fountain-fresh air. I listen, I sing:
O bitter half curl, cirrus of forelock,
dandled and strung with a lark's head knot!

I

V-Winged and Hoary

All our pink and gold and blue
birds have gone to Panama or Peru:

the willow flycatcher with its sneezy "fitzbew,"
the ruby-throated hummingbird with jewel-

like gorgets and the blue-rumped finch,
its song a warble with a guttural "chink."

Far, far across the ghostly frozen lake,
above the great drifts of snow swaying

like dunes, the frosty Iceland gulls,
pallid as beach fleas, make great loops and catfall

into the wind. They are all that is left.
Throngs of children tiptoe deftly

across the lake to watch the robust birds
plunge headlong into kamikaze dives, lured

by fledgling trout nosed against the shallow ice.
Despite the precarious ice,

the children huddle bundled at the edge:
mittened, scarved and starry-eyed,

their teeth chattering in the frosty air.
They watch the tireless birds, over and over,

fall from the speckled sky, their downy underwings
and pink, taloned leggings

7

foam-soaked as they grapple with their catch.
The children are in love with the miraculous

oval-lipped trout swimming upwards for air.
Snowflakes fall against their

cracked lips as they wait, their mouths agape
in little O's at the spectacle of gulls.

The Beavers at Sweet Briar

Big brown bats
course across the lake
gulping insects,

bolting slender
green wasps as they dip
their pendulous

stingers into
the flat, gnat-ridden water,
scouting out

the luckless frog
dozing on the swamp-maple leaf raft,
its beautiful irises

hooded in the half-
light of aquatic life where
a beaver glides

into the night
towing mouthfuls of aspen twigs home
to a litter

of yearling
kits camped in a lodge
on the creek's edge

where clumps
of alder and great tufts of sedges
have sprouted,

and the handsome
native orchids — lady slippers —
are wilting

but whitish
against the sleek beaver furs
hidden . . .

Yes, hidden,
like the brown bat, against the sapling-
ridden slash.

Heart of the Monarch

Lesser fritillaries or crescents might
have lost their tribe in the piedmont,
or some wayward zone, sailing northward like
tiny spinnakers over upper-austral regions

of deciduous hickory and gum,
but near where flat coastal plains
verge westward across forests, overcome
by spring, the African-winged, black-veined

monarchs revive across the temperate,
Mayish sky. Assembling each late noon
for sleep, the young bachelor males alight
in unison, the flash and dazzle of venation

klatched near a pond's muddy crevasse.
This puddle club of monarchs, weary and peaceful,
dozes — unappetizing to the thrasher,
the rough-winged swallow or the needle-

billed hummingbird — abdomens chock-full
of milkweed, foul-tasting to hungry fowl.
So this sleeping assembly, fearless, roosts till
morning when the herd ascends, their spiracles

yawning as they make their way, steadfast.
Out of vivariums, out of seclusion
from under stones and turfy grass, the half-
grown caterpillar emerges; out of unsewn

mats of silk; out of winter lethargy,
the hibernating chrysalis unruffles
its royal self, its larval life a wee
memory; out of the land of nod, adults

begin their lazy, deliberate flights
(The conspicuous *monarchs*, mind you, not
the miniature, mimicking *viceroy!*) —
these flower-eating kings, farsighted,

as they make their way with antennae
precision across the psalm of America
toward Milwaukee and Manitoba.
There's nothing to fret. They're on their way.

Sauna

All the beast within
us is pacific and lame,
    lying flipflop like dragons
    on the cedar frame

as the steam rises softly
above the magic rocks
    that make this little box
    such a convalescent spot.

Haggard and ungroomed,
our cowlicks abloom,
    our trunks and limbs freckled
    with giant dewdrops, the dappled

air ennobles our chests
filling with jets
    of the blessed-baked air,
    our noses rosy and flaring,

until each of us has that
brilliant, pulmonary
    moment when the body cants,
    like a goblet pitched with sherry,

its capillaries singing
their tingling, fragile state,
    and we emerge dehydrated
    and thirsty as frogs sprung

from a dry well, a sudden
zest thundering our spirits
    as we plunge into an icy fountain,
    breathless, goosefleshed and converted.

Coconuts and Pink Pajamas

A turtle-town of Quonset huts
beached in the Blue Ridges of Camp Goshen.
No ocean. Only a watershed
of emotion — all of us pre-acne,

hyperactive, emancipated scouts.
Give it back! — the whir and thud
of an archery lesson, our blunted
arrows like missiles, each of us

a tiny cupid or budding commodore.
Balmy breezes blowing through us,
we Kiwi-shined our bushman boots
and whiptied our tomahawks.

Goosing, guffawing, "Goshenites,"
we merit-badged from bugling
and beekeeping to legumes
and grasses (the resurrection

fern, my ace identification —
a kicker for Tenderfoots!).
Sundown powwows left us bunked,
each with a smoldering tune

or thought or affection, buckshee
stashed in our Keds for post-taps repartee.
And once in my cadet-blue sneaker,
a Carolina wren startled and soaked

from a soppy shower. Raindrops galloped
across our tin hut — Be reverent,
be clean, be strong! — and the wren,
cloaked in my neckerchief,

peeped and shuddered inside my
body-heated Ked until she was dry,
and we could feed her full
of Baby Ruths so she could fly.

Dorothy's Fossils

Ninety million years ago a duck-billed
dinosaur chased and caught a *gillius,*

a fleshy fish of algal blue,
in a sudden, dog-toothed move

that left the fish unhinged, its spine
drifting downward through legions of wine

dark sea into murky bottom waters
where its vertebrae would catch like a spur,

become coated with lime and flourish
in an oysterbed's fertile niche.

Ninety million years later
Dorothy, my childhood mate,

lay serpent-like on a cool field-stone.
The summer's splendor sputtered and shone

all afternoon: Dorothy's freckles diaphanous
in the sunlight, her fragile frock mussed

from our wriggling play. Dorothy lay
in a pool of molten green rays —

her body sunken in a posture of sleep,
her carrot-red hair like sea-lettuce sweeping

above the tall aquatic grass —
when the earth beside her fragile cheek hatched

in the heat of the sun, and the field-stone's
long oppressed trace of Jurassic life untombed

itself before Dorothy, the sleeping child,
who awoke beside the shards of riddled flint,

her heart thrumming like a bird's,
to find the perfect spine unearthed and electric beside her.

The Mare

I remember the shade where I found her
spent and bruised like the fallen apples.
Like them she was full of darkness.
Full of the sweetness which rushes upon us
so soon after death.
She lay there like a mummy,
like the wreckage of an ancient queen,
mild, yet locked away within herself.
It held me the long afternoon —
the secret fruit, the silken mare —
until the day had passed.
I stood and walked among the goats
with their delicate steps
and fed them apples
so mellow
they burst like hearts before the queen and me.

The Biblical Garden
at St. John the Divine in New York City

Everything looked authentic and frail.
And the great clappers of rainfall
made one fancy Noah's ark
drydocked on the lawn, ready to sail.

At the gate were cypress,
the mangy cemetery sort, and beyond
lay the arboretum of the Holy Land.
On a quarter acre it flourished

against the south cathedral choir.
First there were eatables children
longed for in the wilderness.
Then chicory, dandelion and sorrel —

the bitter herbs of their feast.
No matter where you looked there was green
burnished by the thunderhead's stream.
Even the ornamental florets were harvest!:

the blue blossomed flax, a slender erect
annual spun for centuries into linen,
so precious a cropless season
was God's most terrible threat;

the greenish Star-of-Bethlehems'
bulbs trowelled and ground with flour,
their trumpeting lilies christened "dove's dung"
for the pigeons roosting among them;

and the succulent aloe's spicate
flowers — its fleshy foliage yielding
a rainbow of fiery ointments to heal
and embalm the body of Christ.

All afternoon the garden held its breath
against the rain, against the hidden sky.
Ten sleepy cedars of Lebanon — spicy
evergreens timbered for Solomon's temple —

dozed against the holy buttresses.
Beneath their rainless boughs a damp-footed pair
of squirrels hurried over spears
of glistening cedar needles.

The Pharoah's daughters found Moses
adrift in a cradle of papyrus, tipped
in the bulrushes at the lip
of the Nile. *Whose is this?*

they cried, emerging
from the tide, midriff-deep in lather.
Saint John the Baptist, on his hazardous path
through the wilderness of biblical spring,

sandalled, toga-draped and imperial,
craved the carob's pod of sugary pulp.
He doused them each in wild honey, gulping
their golden locust pods whole.

Home, later, in our snug kitchen,
out from the garden's umbrella of fronds,
away from the cathedral's long
exploding verticles, only its thin

Teutonic pinnacles faint on the meridian,
we listen to the rage of the green-gray sky.
An ocean, it slaps its eye
against our fifth floor window rims.

Silly or symbolic it all persists:
the fresh cut grass
springing upwards towards the amassed
clouds; our apple-blossomed teacups

brimming with Darjeeling
and tipped softly against our lips,
filling us with bittersweet sips
of the garden Eastward, into Eden.

Canard

No rapture exceeds driving south in August,
the roof down, someone you love or could love
asleep beside you as you make your way
in a lilliputian car across a mammoth landscape
toward the south, the sea looming like Gulliver in our hearts,
the sun bathing our brows with coronas of pink, with salt,
with the hills hammering past so much that when at last
the aching ball of light overhead falls beneath
the skirt of a cloud, a flock of iron-winged
canards hurrying in a smudge across the horizon
open their bright beaks and give out a hoarse, Miocene honk.
Behold the bronze, wheat-brimming field!
In the windshield an elm-embroidered lane,
an affable farmhouse frozen
as if in a crystal globe, a tiny morality
tale sleepy beneath the cloak of winter's inactivity,
shaken up, made live, made blizzard like alka-seltzer in a glass.
I can hear a couple whispering to one another
as one nuzzles like a pony against the other.
Sunday morning, the coverlet thrown back,
they sleep lightly, waking and dreaming in succession,
their slippers tucked beneath their featherbed,
a fifth of spirits drained in the kitchen.
Their household is snug as a hatbox.
They seem to be poised mid-air, their lives yet unlived.
What they are and what they are not are faultless
as little clouds of breath expel from their chests.
O blurred, delicious tarmac
drawing us toward the strange, pink-sanded sea.
O childish heart. O pleasure drive. O domitable spirit.
Accept! Accept! When the rest of the world is at Z
and you only at C (the central conundrum
of your unhappiness), and you wish to be small

as in every child's fantasy of Swift's island,
small enough to lie in a soup spoon,
just a speck in an ignorant world,
the sweetest revenge is acceptance.
Lap and gurgle at its spoon of escape.
Tug like a squirrel from its mother's teat,
from the rough story, ardent against the joyless moment,
as a father stoops to his child and sees in his eyes
not the rival of a young leopard, but the tenderness of his legacy.
Let the rapture come! — an accordion of dolorous days
squeezed into a sweet rhapsody.
Down the hillside a boy sails with his sheep,
across the trestle a train blazes like a comet,
and in our convertible two shining bodies
glance back at a flock of canards and are carried
south in August toward the strange sea.
Let the rapture have them!

Of Island Animals

It's the lean-legged egrets
which make me think most of risk,
of this tenuous world so near the marshes.

What ruthless lives they lead
alighting each day near a different cow,
their slender bills prodding the center of one's head,

another's spine, preening that small spot
in the herd for a day,
until months have lapsed and these simple birds

have had them all, tasted each in our herd
and abandon this island for another.
That they live such frugal lives is plain

as they lift over our marshes,
their ivory wings folding beside them.
That's how we are: our own lives as tentative.

This morning I think of you everywhere,
of my habit of restlessness,
how I've locked you away from me

and come like the hungry birds
to this island. That I see you
in the faces of small animals

makes me know I must let you go,
that the risk which draws
me here is like a wind:

Once unloosed it spends itself.
For nights I have listened to the wild mink
slinking beneath my cabin, preying

on the remembered taste of his first hen,
her crimped wings, that tender world
which inhabited itself so compactly.

He had our nine hens,
waited a spell, then
returned for the single wild dove

which thrived among them,
the peculiar one to the hungry mink.
That's how our love is:

at first the parted lips
humming and brimming with song,
the quiet middle time,

the eventual abandon.
What the egrets and mink share
is a world that rewards them,

something invented and fresh
each time they return to it,
and hold it in their beaks and jowls.

But it, too, wells before them
like the first remembered world,
the one abandoned so long ago.

Tonight my body is a slip of moon,
a leafy glen in autumn
offering its light to you for nothing.

II

Holiday

Another gemmy beginning:
and so we acquiesce, our fate titanic
as our silver steamer idles and vanishes
into a tunnel of fog.

The first herbage of land brings a cry
from the bow,
guiding us through the ivory gates of cloud
to a green seascape hypnotizing

our sleepless assembly. Beyond lie the floodgates
of land, the sea a spillway through the haze,
as gallant and navigating as a shipmate,
coaching us clear of the straight

spine of a mountain range,
its talus freighted with bird fauna.
And so our tiny steamer puffs along,
drawn by the verdure of spring

into the bay toward the cliff-side
century plants urging us
on with their octopus
arms into the village astride:

Come to the verandah. Have some fruit.
Do not be lured.
We have come away at last.
Take hold! The New World is in our route.

The Octopus Orchid

We sit for hours at the yellow kitchen table
coaxing the sun from her meek position
behind the steeples and masts of this clapboard town.
Now the storm has gone away,
and what should have been a brilliant light,
what should have been all the things we could see,
have squandered themselves in the shower,
in the dripping plush of foliage,
and in the fatigued, impenetrable sky,
hung like stonework above us.

Like the pitiful sun
we linger against the bluish horizon
in the shadows of a kitchen where we can talk,
and conversation is like a cloud
rising eternally against the sun.
I watch the roses trellised against the porch,
how they flare, exulting
as the sun drops free of her captive,
sprays her wild violet beacon across the face of the house,
then wheels into the horizon.

They cluster three abreast
like the sprays latticed into our rose-papered bedroom,
where at night the walls spill in an arbor over us.
When we come at last to the room,
weary, there is a cheerfulness to the walls,
to the scarlet and plum-skinned blossoms,
their faces flocked about us.
How immodest we must look to them, or childlike,
as we slip delighted from our clothes.
What a vulgar beauty we have,
our shallow bellies gleaming like moons beneath the arbor.

I have thought how familiar we must seem to them,
how they must see in us all the lovers
who have stammered across the threshold of this house.

Perhaps if we shouted just once
something odd and mannerless,
the faces would vanish into the pink sky.
It is easy to stay all night there,
awakening once as I always do,
to quench a thirst, to walk,
or to stare out the bathroom window
at the needle-thin steeples and turrets,
at the world which is inexplicable at that hour.
The day would be a pity without these moments.

Last night on the landing
I brushed against the octopus orchid.
Its tentacles seemed to crowd up against me.
It was a bell-shaped mass of stippled mauve.
The scent was sweet and vigorous.
The clumsy arms reached out from their pot,
struggling for the first white flash of sunlight.
It offered a kind of modest miracle,
like the storm-tossed roses,
as if to beckon me back to the make believe arbor.

The Marble Queen

Beneath the whorish scent of magnolia
we watch the parade
spill like a river across the avenue before us.

There in the shade I am the child
whistling at the first tide of soldiers,
their boyish hair cropped beneath berets.

There in the shade is mother,
fixed in her common, girlish pose,
her slim legs tucked beneath her.

She pats the blanket beside her,
dusts a fly from her cheek,
then all at once runs her fingers through her hair

until they catch and snap free into the air.
I watch the blue material of her dress
dimple and lift with each gust of wind.

I am happy, I am sad, dazzled
by the wonderland of uniforms that blurs before us.
Which one is me? Which one is not?

I am the child with his magnifying glass
blazing the hearts from insects
then scattering the skeletal ash.

In the gentle dreams of this child
I could match any battalion at war like a giant
and descend from the heavens on my bean stalk

to monitor the sagging world below.
And once I'd grumbled fitfully,
left the armies bewildered like ants

amidst their hills in the ordinary geraniums,
I would ascend my fertile stalk
towards the moonlight of home.

But mother is thinking of something else —
something beyond the river of men
marching into the pastures of violet

and violet-orange haze where they may fall,
something beyond the young son she has brought
to witness their regaling of strength —

as if the parade has caught her conscience,
and in her conscience, a thousand other women.
Some unforgettable picture wells inside her

until she sees it hovering before her
like the bees and mayflies humming
in the blue afternoon —

there so long, so simple,
she has misunderstood it:
the terrible monotonous despair.

And now she sits alone with it,
finds expression for it like a child
dreaming of shadows, waiting

for her mother and father to shake her from it.
And when all the armies have passed,
only their footsteps faint in the immense sunlight,

she tamps the half-moons of her eyelashes,
rises before me like a marble queen
and seizes herself from it.

Father's Jewelry Box

Home for a weekend retreat
   in the tweezered suburbs with Mother
and her four-columned Colonial
   off Colt's Neck cul-de-sac,
she away at the hairdresser
   near the Giant, I make a snoop
at her done-over bedroom,
   Louis Quinze, the blue catalog ensemble,
lovelorn but lovely, and in the feast
   of father's sleepy chest
of drawers, beneath a rainbow of boxer
   shorts and a pile of bobbed socks,
I find, brassy, fleur-de-lised, and looking-
   glassed, Father's jewelry box.

Caught in a single gasp, the treasure unsnapped,
   the contents a forgotten (forbidden?) potluck:
One copper "BVM," the Mother of Jesus
   faint behind a veil of oxidation,
cozily fastened to Daddy's war-proof
   dog tags worn like a patriarchal
cross across five continents;
   five baby teeth — two cavitied,
two female and three male — plucked
   from each of us tots;
one crystal earring flashing like a javelin;
   monogrammed studs and links for penguin
attire; a Masonic medallion with an eye-
   of-God as sad as a crocodile's;

the vague odor of cologne, of hairbrush,
   of body scent from ribbons starred
and striped; an awful purple heart;

a gold wedding band inscribed in Roman caps:
UNTIL THE LAST — yet never worn as Father
    probed the galvanic gut of machinery,
the ring a volcanic conductor of electricity
    inducing cardiac arrest.
All this to the tune of "Star Dust,"
    its melody lulling as Mother arrives
coiffed from the Giant, her bosom breathless
    as she catches me by surprise: "Good Heavens!" —
But I am neither, pirating an oyster's pearl from her room,
    my head fogged with the scent of her perfume.

The Prince Enters the Forest

full of courage and promise like the geese gone away,
his horse trembling beneath him on the trail of burr.
He cannot, despite all that he will spare her,
bring his thoughts from her continuous sleep, so he prays,

now and again embarrassed by her,
imagining her dress half opened from decay,
the coat of dust at her lips — which will he touch first? —
her sewing hand fallen like a bird from its cage,

the red bead still fluttering on its bill.
Will he kiss her lids or raise them
and touch each astonished iris, shrunken and still?
Will she sleep on and on in her kingdom of thorn,

or will the world catch in her heart, in his mouth,
and rage like the geese overhead, warring south?

Found Sonnet on a Postcard from Milwaukee

My problems with Monty have abated.
The elms are shaken, the lake is a desert of frost,
and I'm sleeping with allergy pills. Kyoko's mismated
with a landscape-painter. Her tears are prodigious,
though she's a perfect housemate: I'm writing sonnets.
Chris is studying and his teeth are fixed.
All these separations! Have you forgotten?
Nuala is nuts over Spain. Bewitched!
I'm not mooning anymore. Monty's so
withdrawn that I can let him ignore me.
A kind of golden age, though all my own.
I needed something to be proud of. Agreed?
Just finished a dish of noodles which
recall those days in '78. Anyway, you're missed.

The Limo–Angel

Zigzagwise across the beltway,
awash with pinkish
effulgence from taillights
and paralysis —

our Spider Fiat,
"as sound as a roach,"
inching homeward, caught
in the holiday (HO-

LY day?) exodus
on a rain-hammered night,
when its 4-cylinders percussed
and stalled — we guide

our ailing roach
roadside through a tangle of Pintos
and Gremlins and Impalas,
the rain spattering

its accordion roof
like a thin-shelled pullet's egg.
If there is Providence it looked
upon us at the highway's edge,

down-parkaed and sober,
traffic feathering past
our rain-sopped impasse,
when a limousine approached

from the throng, its sleek
obsidian door swung open.
Chastened and pink-cheeked,
we hopped in.

The chauffeur smiled at his
dreamlike date in a panther skin,
then turned our way
offering a flute of champagne.

We sipped. Then they sipped.
He said, *It's the King's.*
He's out tonight, the panther said.
Delivered home bubbleheaded,

we wished the strangers
and their King well,
then our limo zipped past a manger
fixed on a rooftop's swell.

Diana and the Adder

are asleep daintily on the lawn,
neither one revived
beneath the sun's boiling eye.
    The afternoon presses forward around them,
        cheerful, despite its crazy spire of heat and light.
          Above the flowerbed's cadenza of zinnias,
          bonnets of sunflowers
          bow their heads in rebuke,
        woeful for Diana, whose abandon
        enchants the dotted serpent
    rising from its knot of sleep.
The two of them are there like summer,
twin anatomies bellydown,
    capsized, each impassable to the other.
        Diana's novel is open to a climactic
          chapter marked with a dandelion
            before her digression,
              its yellow blossom like the viper's
              iridescent spots — What harm can come to her? —
    the novel compressing itself into her revery
of a woman opening shutters like the wings of a novel
onto a glittering slate roof,
her blue dressing gown loose around her
    as she stretches out on a sofa
        and reads beneath the whitish vapor of a lamp
        that seems to cast a spell on her,

and on the reader, Diana,
where she lies unaware of the sequined
serpent. You can see its belly breathing,
unhandled and jointless,
its heart a classic motor pulsing in the grass.
Come from some terrestrial heartland,
hog-nosed and stout-bodied,
it moves assuredly close to Diana,
its transparent eyelids blinking,
its binocular eyes rolling backwards
inside their nodules,
its single-spiked tongue
hissing with a cruel flicker
as Diana rises suddenly,
letting out a ferocious spasmodic yawn
that sends the carnivorous creature, alarmed,
mousing into a bigtoothed thicket,
and Diana back to her alluring protagonist,
her tiny blue irises reflecting in miniature
the pages before her as she delves
beneath their tonic
spell.

III

Desert Days on the Reservoir

Talking town but always
   thinking Christ! Christ!
Silly me, a hick
   in an evening jacket,

guest at a neighbor's
   pint-sized, terrace-lipped
house, a Trinity
   home of feathered brick —

Trinity, minus the Father
   and Spirit, ALL of us
sons (and sonless!)
   watching the sun go down

like a baby's head
   upon a vista of summer
and a jetsam of sultry air.
   Watch the rising stars,

brightest Vega on the zenith,
   a mica point
on a noiseless reservoir,
   where a terrapin glides

bankward, a speck of green,
   its flesh cozy
inside a diamondback,
   its horny beak wet-fresh

from a lunch of liquid grass.
Now the speedboats,
breathless from their day
of bouncing across the lake,

are snug in their slips,
their engines propped
across their bows
like the heads of sunbathers,

and the turtle makes its way,
even now delirious
from the trough and chop
of their wake.

From scent to scent:
fumes from my tumbler of sweet
wine, the gillyflowers' aroma
of clove beyond the terrace,

the squeak of sexuality,
that ancient power
breaching our enclave of toms
with its pirate of thirst.

Beneath a sky of aquatint,
I do not know
my destination and watch
the smoke pour from my

neighbor's lips like a sonnet
of foam written
against the evening's
late glimmer of sunlight.

Like animals at the zoo,
   we lounge and loll
in a world of seeming
   purity that leaves us dreaming,

all of us neat, prosaic
   figures reposed against these
desert days on the reservoir;
   all of us on the edge

of madness and effervescence,
   imagining ourselves
very near to heaven,
   despite the catalog of sins

behind us, and the peacock's
   imperious voice in each of us,
tiny as a sparrow, calling:
   "Catch the rising stars!"

Patroclus: A Love Song

I have been thinking of the son I might have had,
how before I died I saw him twice:

First his head was reared,
caught in a wild, astonished tick,
and at last, it rested in my lap,

his ear cupped in my hand like a secret.
I wanted to crawl inside his flesh
so that when he wandered

or alone at night felt moored by the darkness,
I would feel my own organs snug within his
and could hold him by the shoulders.

When he grew old I would still be there
flowing with the sweet juices from his heart,
imperfect and precious like a pearl.

Tonight I lie awaiting Iris' return from the valleys
where the North and West winds have promised a gift.
They will rouse themselves this evening

to fan the blaze where I will burn.
She tells them to wait for evening, for the moon,
which tonight is hesitant and pale.

She tells them I will let go now.
First they boil a sweet mixture of wine.
Then they bathe me, rinse the blood clots

and rub nard into my open wounds.
They set me on a bed of linen, soft as lambskin.
Thetis, your mother, fills my nostrils

with nectar to keep my body whole,
to keep the flies from settling on my spearwounds.
They rub and oil my body with ambrosia.

Twice they anoint me with rose oil.
My skin will never rot!
Touch me. Touch me.

For days they have foraged firewood,
trimmed and split the trunks,
then stacked them like kindling beneath me.

I am the eye of their pyramid.
Their fragile empire pulses beneath me.
I am not alone: first sheep and cattle,

their organs propped like cushions against me.
Then the great collapsed horses.
I am deep in their rumpled shadows.

Tonight the air is blue like the veins in a lamb's neck.
I am slender and mild as that lamb.
Your men have come to me for hours.

They lament and cover me
with their sheared locks like petals.
One among them with his red-gold hair

opened my hand and set it there.
I think of the lioness returning after her long hunt
to a den, itself the object of a hunt.

How she grieves and meanders the valleys
for the tracks of the hunter.
Now I am left alone. At last entirely forgotten.

I will burn so quickly, lovely like a failed letter.
First the down on my arms will raze itself.
My fingers will light, curl like hooks, then falter.

My lungs and diaphragm will expand
until suddenly I rise,
my chest and shoulders leaning forward into the moon.

And there as I sit with my great moon eyes
looking out over the open sea, over the galewinds
that blast the fire beneath me,

my tongue for a moment will unwither itself,
will lap and twitch in its mouthful of honey.
It will be like lying down before love,

each of us caught by something exquisite
in the other's unexpected release.

Midnight Sailing on the Chesapeake

The lavish canopy of crape myrtles
branching across the avenue;
the four Hatteras conches, tuned
to different seas and curled

like gazelle tines upwards from the masts
of my bedposts where I hung them —
mementos of summers peerless and past;
the columns of endless rain,

condensed from clouds, brutal and black
above our town as they crashed
against the sleeping porch
where I dozed beneath the arch

of our wind-gnashed willow,
my eyelids and cheeks swollen
from the milky haze of Virginia pollen;
the plush of mother's phlox

cascading across the granite garden walks;
my teenage self, a unit of boundless
energy, harnessed like steam or a river: all this
as contents in a first night's sleep

with my father on his sloop.
I have returned to visit him,
ail-stricken but convalescing, amused
by his heart, a bypassed facsimile

of my own, his panacea,
an earthless season on the Chesapeake,
a diet of bluepoints and brine,
and he'll slip into Septuagenaria.

This is how the prodigal began — or ended? —
guiltless and favored until his heart
burned and filled with malefaction.
So peaceful is the black night, the black sea,

spreading its velvet acreage like a forest
limitless before us.
We let the sails luff,
empty of wind, then come about,

tacking once, twice through the mouth
of St. Mary's hairpin south.
Far off on a promontory the beacon
of a home blinks twice, twice again,

warning us of the unlikely isthmus,
the rocky shallows where tiny vessels
like our own batter and dash their keels.
Father says an aged seaman is the river's eye;

from his crow's nest at the rocky lip of the St. Mary
he pilots the home bound into western estuaries.
In the moonlight my father is brilliant,
an Incan god, his gray curls

blazing with salt and starlight.
He watches the black-hearted Chesapeake
sweep away behind us, the eastern sea
swelling and throbbing like the heart of a child.

The rudder churns a tilth of foam
rising in a wave behind us, ever
tracing our wanderlust from home,
our windy romantic endeavor.

We set out two days ago,
the sky a bell around us,
its tongue the compass for our journey
into the gulf, into the burning dusk.

In the first day's light we followed
the sun until she fell like a bird
across the pines, swallowed
in the August horizon without a word.

Father's sloop is "Ajax" — not the Lesser! —
a wave-worn, square-sterned vessel,
its standing bowsprit, a javelin aloft.
Our lighthearted dinghy is "Raindrop,"

her blue fiberglass shell
like a tear wept from the sea,
spangled in the black air. She flails
in the wake of Ajax, in the pearl-dark sea.

We cannot swim or think to swim
in this season of nettles and jellyfish.
When in the flashlight I beam them,
their saucerlike hulks, rich

in phosphorus, shrink and shudder.
They collect against our lanternlit sloop,
wrap their tentacles about the rudder.
We must cast the stewpot out and scoop

a bailful of creatureless sea to cool
ourselves, father and I, on the prow
where we shiver and howl like fools
from the blasts of icy water down

our spines, expectant and bowed.
The sails shimmer and furl in a sudden gust.
The deck heels into the sea its crescent brow,
spraying a lace of ocean across us.

Father and I are silent in the shaken air.
I pencil him into a craggy sketch —
a figure against the sea — unaware
that my view askance can catch

him like an ancient bird.
If I could lift a word
I'd lift it faithfully towards him.
I would sigh a long lion-like sigh at first,

as if to start a lion-like tale
and then recount the story of the prodigal —
of the willful son and the son without will.
If I could lift a word as full

and fine as he would wish,
I would offer to join him in his journey
through the salt-edged gate of clipper and fish.
We watch the signs from the east,

the curious signals of squall:
The moon, moody and weary-eyed
coaxes the flaming stars to fall,
to turn their faces from our sight.

We drop anchor in an uncharted, coverted cove,
let the main and jib fall
and wrap them in their cozies,
then await the ranting thundersquall.

The birds in the trees tighten their bills.
The embers in the grill spit and spark.
Our hull takes each breaker as it fills
with wind and billows like a satin scarf.

The blue mackerel descend to the grassy bay floor.
The amphibious ducks bob their heads in the current,
raindrops storming against them, content
as they paddle towards their defended shore.

The land's sharp features lose their detail.
The tremulous squall delays herself a bit,
lets the sky turn rose, aqua, then sable,
then blasts ecstatically her sinister fit.

Father descends into the hold of Ajax,
stows the jib and stokes the lanterns,
stoic against the threshold of tempest and morass.
I sit astern and witness the flashing nocturne.

Tomorrow it will be a perfect, clear day.
Indian princesses who once bathed
on the distant opalescent rocks
will seem nearer than their centuries away.

The air will be clear of everything.
I will oar "Raindrop" across the cove,
beyond the sea urchins' sting,
to the sacred bathing spot and dive

into the many-shouldered fragrant day,
my skin brown as an Indian's
against the azure bay.
Father, in seeing me off to an early swim,

will set himself to his daily chores.
Whistling a snatch of an old tune,
he oils the teak, parched and weatherworn,
and pitches the tarpaulin across the boom.

After swimming for hours in the pure morning air,
plunging and gliding like an otter across the lagoon,
I lift myself onto the great gray rocks, and there
in the miraculous sun a teaspoon

of light shines up from the water
like a crystal whirling with color from the sky.
Thunderbolts the night before
have left a tumbling and hissing tide.

Miniature crabs scrabble across the granite,
their tiny hearts wheezing with oxygen.
Starlings circle overhead, their appetites
delighted by the ill-tempered crustaceans.

Little by little the light flicks
its queer ray in my eyes. Stirred,
I stretch out beneath the erratic
sunlight, beneath the umbrella of firs.

I think of the world disassembling itself
for the start of another season,
or of the black forests delving
across the peninsulas beyond,

or of the Indian princesses,
their gooseflesh trembling in the surf.
How contented and ageless they seem,
like father drowsing beneath his canopy,

his pinched heart released like a buoy into the bay.
He looks at the ocean around him.
Everyone is gone except for me.
In the teaspoon of light he is just a boy,

like his son with the surf in his heart.
He dips his tennis shoes into the sea,
splashing his calves and knees.
We cannot tell ourselves apart.

The Nectar and Semen of Change

If I were a shepherd with flocks
grazing beneath the willows,
my boyish thoughts would dart with the finches,
plummeting from the highest heaven of poplars
to the earth-bound honeysuckle.
I would exist exactly as I do —
imagining the finch as some part of myself,
and in the densest ring of willow
I would give myself up,
taking the disguise of finch for my soul.

The world would be a blur at first
encompassed by the immensity of sky,
but from my nest at the apex of the forest
I'd watch the spring unfurl around me,
each new leaf burning outward in its discovery
of white and yellow sunlight.
And it would be all right there alone at night
beneath the black infinite dome.
Raising my eyes toward a crowd of constellations,
each night there would be something new:

Heaven, a mere wonder beyond the sun
to my mortal shepherd self,
would press against the treetops
as real as the poplar's yellow tulips.
Some nights I might ascend into the starlit heaven
sweeping beyond the weightless bats
to an open clearing where angels
might receive my soul in its disguise of finch,
still dizzy from the spiraling upward flight,
into the great calm of their wings.

I would float all night there
singing outwardly as if to lullaby
the drowsy shepherd and his flocks below,
and there I would see the mastery of spring,
the nectar and semen of change.
The young shepherd sprawled lizard-like in the grass
would lift his eyes at the glittering light of moon and stars,
his body shuddering from the moist meadow.
He'd believe he has risen to begin the long journey
through the hills where his sheep will lose their fleece,

but it's seduction and the great confusion of spring
that draws him into the night toward us.
His most perfect desire is to hold me,
to have me perch on his powerful hand.
If at day I see him cooling beneath the willows,
little streams of sweat shuddering across his chest,
I will alight on his wrist and rub my beak,
glistening with oil from the calm
angelic atmosphere, across his palm.

My Sweetest Lesbos

Erratic fruit-bats
rattle across the moon-shafted sky,
haphazard and zigzagged

as the lizards
that scuttle across this barren, bonsai
paradise. Eastward

the Milky Way
and its myriad clusters electrify,
make shimmer the night

above distant
summerhouses, their slippery red roof-tiles
lustrous on the horizon

beneath the scorpion's
segmented stinger of stars. Despite
terrestrial lights,

despite the sweet,
beguiling night, we return to our seaside,
Spartan rooms, to our screaking

cast iron beds
resting against the wall like giant spiders;
past the shed

of spearfishermen,
their gangly, sinewy bodies excited
and unloosed

from their gleaming black
wetsuits like newborn, galvanic butterflies;
past the village

idiot, his face
pinched and boyish as he hikes
his slacks to his waist

and draws his belt
another notch; past the steaming, allspiced
kitchen where a native uncoils

from an oily bucket
a ghastly, quivering eel plied
from the Aegean and twisting

like a worm enriched
from the black earth; past the green hillsides
velvety as yellowjackets,

veiled in curtains
of trembling olive groves; past the high-
spirited, teen-driven

Vespas sprinting
their magic expectant hearts along side
the embattled coast;

past the jack-o-lantern
music of tavernas glowing like satellites;
past the Hotel Delphian

pool, its cool
green ring dazzling and lunar-bright
with sunflowers, dahlias

and pinkish oleander
bobbing around its hemisphere of saltwater
in which a bikini-clad

woman glides, dolphinry,
through the aquamarine Aegean light
till she bursts

through the surface
like a mermaid clambering ashore, her icy
hair and breasts

shaken loose from the tide,
her limbs bewebbed like the mosquito-bats
hovering overhead,

her spine S-shaped
and chameleon-like as she reclines poolside
and spews

a fountain
of seawater into the black night,
full-pulsed

as we walk
hot-faced into the everlasting, pine-
clad, Lesbian hills.

The Buoyant Ending

On an evening slumberous as this
when even the sparrow's song is mum
    at the font where they drink and rut
in the glade, and the phantom
    wind declines its glacial jets
of breath, and the sombre heart of November
    fogs our heads with recall of brilliant
umbrellas, picnic baskets and babies filling
    the shore in midmost May,
a constitutional down the privet-hedged lane
    gives the heart a buoyant lift.
Beneath the shooting sparks of stars,
    beneath the harsh blue night,
a neighbor's hens cluck and titter
    inside their moon-shaded cottage.
You can hear them peck and smart one another
    like queens till their coop is rife
with feathers, and the frowsy mothers
    snuggle their bellies into nests
that quiver as beast eggs, white or rust,
    lodge inside them, fallen
into these latter days of fall
    with logs on the hearth and the earth
rattling with charred leaves, and memory
    blazing like McIntosh apples.
In a horned patch of grass beyond the coop,
    two pups tussle with one another,
one fleeing, the other swatting with its forepaw.
    They spar, ambushing and capering,
with their mouths half open, galumphing
    through the glassy grass, until one lopes
away, and they stop their combat to wash
    one another with long panting-pink tongues,

their hearts thumping from their murderous play.
This is where it begins — after twilight,
with the archer's arrow winking from its Southern
Hemisphere, with the clear eye of each planet
vigilant against the rooftopped night,
with the plumpest squirrels falling deeply,
beneath comforters of acorns, toward sleep —
the buoyant hope that in a month,
or many, the fog will lift,
that these twig-bound days will open
their capacious hearts into an apogee of summer,
that our fleshy pets will grow lean again,
that our reticent lips will hurl with phrase,
and that the empty zone of winter will turn
restless like the sea and fume
with landscape, with maze, with sultry sun:
all of it like a bronzed boy, the opiate of hope.
I'm going home. The wind will lift soon.
O the biding, the precious price of summer.
And then you're in the heat of it!